CREATING YOUR FUTURE AFTER A TOXIC RELATIONSHIP

When you find yourself alone after a relationship breakdown and the future you once had planned has evaporated, where and how do you start to create a new future? This book can be used by the reader individually or with a life coach alongside, to support the individual in creating the first steps towards a new future and a 'road map' on how to get there.

Dee Wilkinson uses a coaching approach throughout the workbook, taking the reader through a logical 10-step process to design a brighter future that will be in line with their authentic self. There are exercises, tools and techniques for the reader to work through to help them understand themselves fully, therefore creating better long-term decision making. A life coach can also use the resource to support the reader's journey through the steps by asking coaching questions and offering insights and challenges as necessary to keep the reader on track.

Many texts are aimed at helping people understand the psychology of why they were in a relationship, whereas this workbook enables people to take tangible steps to move on with their lives. It will be of great help to individuals seeking to move on from toxic relationships, as well as life coaches and other mental health professionals.

Dee Wilkinson is an established coach and supervisor and has been practising for over 17 years. She has successfully created her own desired future after a relationship breakdown, by using the tools and techniques in this workbook.

"Dee's personal insight blended with her expertise and experience has developed this brilliant resource to inform and support professionals and individuals alike. The book encourages survivors of abuse to attain their aspirations using a flexible process to meet their personal goals. Highly recommended."

–**Sue Mellor**, MA, Sue Mellor Coaching and Consultancy

"An invaluable workbook for use after the breakdown of an abusive relationship, to help rebuild your confidence and self-worth. The author explores Life Planning in easy to follow, practical steps through a series of exercises. The book empowers the individual to plan for their future and focus on the positive."

–**Kathryn Moggs**, Family Solicitor

"It is all too easy to lose sight of who YOU are in a toxic relationship. This book enables you to take simple, powerful and effective steps towards recovery. Your past does not need to dictate your future. Dee's professional experience and personal insight forms a perfect balance in this easy to follow recovery tool. Learn to love yourself again, learn to take back control and free yourself once more."

–**B.C support worker**, Women's Refuge

CREATING YOUR FUTURE AFTER A TOXIC RELATIONSHIP

A COACHING WORKBOOK

Dee Wilkinson

Routledge
Taylor & Francis Group

LONDON AND NEW YORK

First published 2022
by Routledge
2 Park Square, Milton Park, Abingdon, Oxon OX14 4RN

and by Routledge
605 Third Avenue, New York, NY 10158

Routledge is an imprint of the Taylor & Francis Group, an informa business

© 2022 Dee Wilkinson

The right of Dee Wilkinson to be identified as author of this work has been asserted by her in accordance with sections 77 and 78 of the Copyright, Designs and Patents Act 1988.

British Library Cataloguing-in-Publication Data
A catalogue record for this book is available from the British Library

Library of Congress Cataloging-in-Publication Data
Names: Wilkinson, Dee, author.
Title: Creating your future after a toxic relationship: a coaching workbook / Dee Wilkinson.
Description: Abingdon, Oxon; New York, NY: Routledge, 2022. | Includes bibliographical references.
Identifiers: LCCN 2021020680 (print) | LCCN 2021020681 (ebook) | ISBN 9781032001012 (hardback) | ISBN 9781032000985 (paperback) | ISBN 9781003172734 (ebook)
Subjects: LCSH: Separation (Psychology) | Interpersonal relations. | Man-woman relationships. | Self-perception. | Self-esteem. | Personal coaching.
Classification: LCC BF575.G7 W5555 2022 (print) | LCC BF575.G7 (ebook) | DDC 155.44–dc23
LC record available at https://lccn.loc.gov/2021020680
LC ebook record available at https://lccn.loc.gov/2021020681

ISBN: 978-1-032-00101-2 (hbk)
ISBN: 978-1-032-00098-5 (pbk)
ISBN: 978-1-003-17273-4 (ebk)

DOI: 10.4324/9781003172734

Typeset in Palatino and Scala Sans
by Newgen Publishing UK

Contents

Illustrations

FIGURES

TABLES

A note to coaches

This workbook has been written with the end user in mind to provide a framework that individuals can use to self-coach towards a preferred future. In addition, it is an excellent resource for coaches to recommend to their clients when structuring a programme of life-coaching sessions. As a coach, you can guide, question, support and challenge your clients to commit to actions throughout the workbook to help them on their journey.

The workbook can also be used as a resource for anyone wanting to create a more fulfilling future.

Preface

This workbook was originally formulated in 2013, but I never quite finished it and life moved on as it does. However, we are currently living through the extraordinary time of the Covid-19 pandemic. My heart sank when I became aware of the growing evidence for how many people would be suffering from higher rates of domestic abuse due to the lockdown situation in homes all over the United Kingdom, and globally. Ultimately, this would lead to the breakdown of many relationships worldwide, which created the urgency within me to finalise this book, with the hope that if it could even help one person rebuild their life, then it would have been a worthwhile and small contribution to others in such a difficult time.

As a result of my own experience and learning, I would like to share with you some helpful tools that I used to re-define and create a more rewarding life for myself. In fact, I used it to create a totally new life that was more purposeful, content and of greater value. I am not an expert in domestic abuse or violence, or a trained counsellor or psychotherapist. I am a qualified life, executive and organisational coach, which has given me the skills and insight to create a life that I could only previously have dreamed of, after my own very personal and painful breakdown of a relationship.

WHY A COACHING APPROACH?

All the skills you may have attained as a result of the relationship, such as emotional intelligence, sensing congruency and people watching, can now be used to their full advantage in helping you to move forward in your life.

Counselling is great for putting the past where it needs to be, in the past. There are many tools available to help us get ourselves back on track and they all hold a valuable place in recovery.

There was a point in my life when I felt like I had lost everything, including my home, sense of self and my future.

The future I had planned no longer existed and, for me, staring into what I would describe as 'no man's land' was frightening. I felt an urgency to create a future vision for myself and my family so that we could get back on track as quickly as possible. That meant I needed to start looking ahead rather than behind me.

After retraining as a personal coach, and now a corporate and executive coach, I am testament to the way that our thinking can change our lives or keep us stuck. I found the tools learned in a coaching approach to be extremely effective, giving me back the 'steering wheel' to my life. Coaching is all about looking to the future and working forwards. It differs from counselling that looks to the past, mentoring that is based on another's experience, and advice and consultancy, which is more about an expert coming into a situation for a limited period. A coach believes in you 100 per cent and is committed to your own resourcefulness, believing you have the answers you need already inside you. A coach will not be advising you on what you should be doing but asking you the right questions that will help move you forward.

I really want to share some of the tools and techniques that I have learned, to help you create a bright future that can meet your expectations and to offer strategies to keep it that way. The journey is not necessarily quick and easy, and I have learned that anything worth having rarely is. However, coaching creates small, incremental and achievable steps that help you along your journey. The art is to realise that every small consistent step will be taking you into a more rewarding future, even when sometimes you may feel like you have not come very far. The reward for that effort on my part is now a life of happiness, contentment and inner peace, and I very much wish the same for you.

HOW TO USE THIS BOOK

This practical workbook takes you through a series of 10 steps, which are most effective if taken in order. Each step builds on the last to help you gain the foundations, confidence and direction towards planning a new future. You can work through it in your own time and at your own pace. It may also help to engage a personal life coach or someone you can trust to work through it with you. Think of me as your virtual coach, with you every step of the way. There are icons included in the text to prompt when it is helpful to take an action, take time to reflect or use a practical tool of support. It will be helpful to have your own notebook, but you can also note things down in the spaces provided as you go along. This will create your own personal record of your progress that you can look back on as you achieve your goals.

Table 0.1: Key to icons

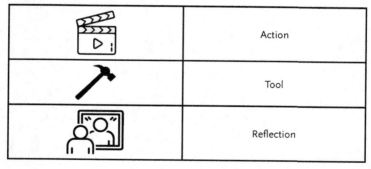

	Action
	Tool
	Reflection

I hope it is helpful and becomes part of your journey. This workbook offers a structure to hang a life on which is fulfilling, passionate, bright, positive, happy and full of love. Know that you really do have the power within you.

Wishing you hope for a new and more fulfilling future and that you find peace within yourself. When I say fulfilling future, this could be as simple as living a life without fear. Never give up, seek help if you need to, and keep on keeping on.

Asking for help is one of the bravest things you can do for yourself

Much love, Dee
Dartmoor 2021

About the author

Dee Wilkinson is the founder and director of South West Coaching, specialising in coaching medical doctors, executive coaching, coaching supervision, and the training of internal coaches and mentors. She has an MSc in Coaching and Development and is an experienced executive coach, coach supervisor, manager, trainer and facilitator.

Dee has worked with the NHS for 22 years and was one of the first to introduce coaching formally into the NHS in Devon in 2004. She has experience of leading innovative teams, transforming working methods, building personal skills and inspiring people. She founded South West Coaching in 2009 and has worked independently since 2011. She is a Master Coach accredited with the European Mentoring and Coaching Council and has been a qualified coach since 2004. Dee's personal coaching interest is in managing personal energy and supporting men and women to meet more of their potential. Publications include *Goal Setting Made Easy* (Wilkinson, 2012) and *Practical Leadership in Nursing and Health Care* (Henwood, 2014). She lives on Dartmoor where, in addition to coaching, she runs a hill farm and livery business with her husband.

Acknowledgements

Thank you to my wonderful family, my husband who is my rock and my unfaltering friends, especially Sandy and Sally who have been by my side on my journey. To Debbie Fisher, a fantastic coach, and Nicole Johnston who founded Collective Wisdom of the Writing Tribe, both who acted as catalysts to making this a reality. Brittany White and my team at work, who without I would not have been able to free up the time. Julie Willis of River Editorial for her unending patience, support and editing skills, and to all that have believed in the value of this workbook.

Taking stock

INTRODUCTION

This Step encourages you to reflect on your life and take stock of your current situation before beginning your journey towards creating a new future. The wheel tool introduced later in the chapter enables you to create a personalised and measurable benchmark of where you are now so that you can measure your success on your journey.

Before you start on any journey it is a good idea to understand where you are starting from. At least then you can measure how far you have come!

I am aware that for a lot of people after the breakdown of a relationship, it can take time to re-discover who you are and what your personal preferences might be. For many, when you are first alone you can be left with no real sense of self. When a relationship ends it can knock your self-confidence, your decision-making abilities, self-esteem and body image, all of which can feel at rock bottom. If you have suffered constant criticism, emotional bullying and belittling tactics, your sense of everything can become very distorted. You may have been constantly shaping your world to satisfy another. Your sense of self then becomes determined by what you are receiving. However, once realised, the only way is up! Once free you may not have any idea of your own likes and dislikes – do you like cross stitch, the colour pink or even mountain biking? It can, and does, take time to recover from a toxic relationship and to become fully well and functioning again. But you can become strong and focused once more, maybe at an even greater level than you ever expected.

DOI: 10.4324/9781003172734-1

Prior to creating a great big action plan, it is important to take stock of exactly how you are.

HOW ARE YOU FEELING?

Are you well? Have you recovered enough, physically and emotionally, to the point where you are ready to move on with your life?

It is important that you have had the opportunity to process the emotions that you will have been affected by. This workbook is written on the basis that you have been able to do this, preferably with a trained psychological professional, and you are now ready to move on in your life. Assuming you are in a good place and are ready to start, we can begin by exploring a series of tools that have been incredibly helpful to me and my clients in taking stock of where they are now. It will help if you use each tool and technique as you go along.

It is a good idea to get in tune with how you are feeling daily. You may not have spent much time listening to your own body's needs, including feelings of tiredness, hunger or needing relaxation. Many individuals who find themselves in the situation of domestic abuse or a toxic relationship tend to put others first. Learning to recognise your own needs without feeling selfish is part of the journey.

JOURNALING

Writing down your thoughts and feelings can help enormously. This is a way of getting the emotion outside of you and can be quite powerful. Buy a lovely empty book/notepad that you like and use it to write out your worries, hopes, fears, thoughts and feelings that have appeared that day. This can help externalise our thinking.

LABELLING EMOTIONS

Labelling our emotions as and when we feel them has been researched as a positive way to manage emotion and retain equilibrium (Rock, 2009). For example: I feel sad. Write it down and then reflect where the sadness is coming from and feel the emotion. It is ok to grieve when we have lost something. Some people are afraid of writing down a word for fear they will feel overwhelmed. However, the research suggests otherwise and explains that just by evidencing what we are feeling with one word can help lower the emotional response and allow our brain to maintain a link with the thinking part.

Learn to recognise your feelings and observe them instead of shutting them away. While it is important to keep focused on the future it is also important to allow yourself to feel connected with what you are really feeling. Go with it and know it will pass. Be your own observer of emotions, thoughts and feelings. If you have not been able to properly process the emotion of any trauma or negative experience, your emotions could feel overwhelming. In this case I would recommend seeking help from a physchotherapist or credible counsellor if you are still in this place and unable to move forward. More about this in the chapter on self-care.

WRITE DOWN HOW YOU ARE FEELING ABOUT YOURSELF

- What is your general mood?
- Are you feeling ready for a challenge?
- Are you still feeling fragile?
- Are you feeling strong emotionally, mentally and physically?

WRITE DOWN HOW YOU WANT TO BE AND WHAT THE BEST VERSION OF YOURSELF WOULD BE LIKE

- What would you be doing?
- What would you look like?
- What would you hear yourself saying?
- What would you be wearing?
- What would others be saying about you (positive only, based on your future desired state).

Creating a vision of how you want to be allows your subconscious to start to support you in achieving it. It does not matter if you are unable to answer all the questions just yet. This is work in progress and you can come back to this. (This may feel difficult if you believe you are not currently like who you want to become or have lost a sense of yourself.) Be kind to yourself and come up with a version that feels comfortable for you. This is about regaining more of who you are, not turning you into something you are not.

 WHEEL OF LIFE

The wheel is a great tool that enables you to take stock of where you are now in your life and create a starting point from which to move forward. The concept of the wheel was first attributed to Paul J. Meyer (1960) and there are now many versions in use. To work towards a well-balanced and happy life you first need to know how you currently feel about your life as it is now. Our lives can be made up of many different areas. Some of the following may apply: family, children, health, finances, relationship, work, environment (where we live), hobbies, job, religion, friends, fun.

This tool helps you to break down and identify the important areas of your life. You can then use it to create a score of satisfaction within each segment. (The most common criteria are scoring against your current level of satisfaction, but you can change the criteria to different things.) You can then use the wheel as a gauge of measurement against your progress and as a foundation for goal setting.

LABEL YOUR WHEEL

The wheel is divided into eight segments. Label each segment with one key area of your life as it is now. It may be that there is currently less than eight areas in your life, and part of this process is to build on that. If you have more than eight, then you can split a segment in half. Try to keep to the top headings. What matters is that they are relevant to you and your life and not what someone else thinks they should be. I have included a blank example wheel here (Figure 1.1.) but it will be best if you draw this out on an A4-size piece of

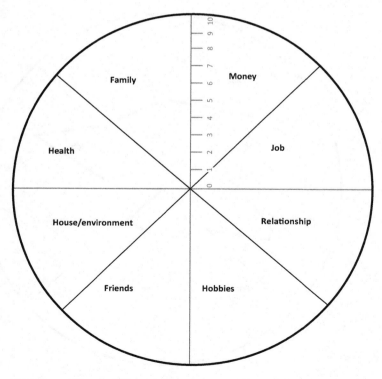

Figure 1.1: Wheel of life template

paper. (Example only – label your own segments to reflect what is relevant to you.)

SCORE YOUR WHEEL

Next, score each segment in terms of your personal satisfaction along the spoke from the centre outwards. The number one would be at the centre of the wheel and 10 on the external radius. A score of one would be the least satisfied and 10 the most satisfied. Mark along each spoke of the segment how satisfied you are with this area. Finally, join up the scores with a line that flows through each segment, creating a new inner wheel as in the example given in Figure 1.2.

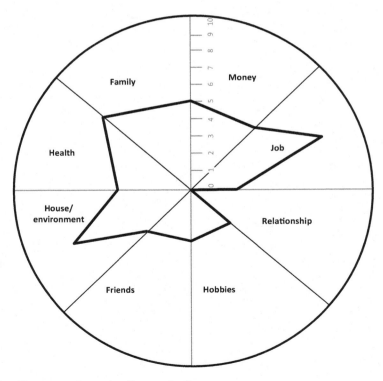

Figure 1.2: Example of inner wheel

LOOK AT THE BALANCE

Study your wheel of life for a moment and see how balanced or unbalanced your life currently feels. If this were a wheel on a car, what sort of ride would you be having? Does the shape of your inner wheel reflect how life feels for you right now?

We will be coming back to this wheel a little later to show you how you can build your level of satisfaction in each of the areas.

STEP 2

How our brain can help us

INTRODUCTION

This Step gives an overview of how the brain functions and how it is activated into survival mode. It helps you to understand the internal processes being triggered in the brain in response to keeping you safe. It looks at helping you to challenge unhelpful thinking habits that may be keeping you stuck and offers a case study outlining an example of how this can be put into practice.

Before we focus on what we do want, it may be helpful if I explain a bit about how the brain works and why we feel the way we do. One of the questions I asked myself was why I felt like I might just die if the relationship ended (apart from the obvious if we are in an abusive relationship where there can be a very real threat to our lives). Also, I was curious to know if I could change the type of relationship that I was drawn to by changing my thinking.

Part of my own confusion was trying to understand why it was so difficult to leave an unhealthy relationship. I also had the knowledge that someone is rarely all bad and often someone's intention is not always how their behaviour is displayed. For anyone in a difficult relationship, if the person they were with was entirely bad I am sure they would find it a lot easier to leave. However, my experience has been that partnerships can have incredibly good parts but, sadly, these parts can be equally matched with parts that are not helpful. This makes it much harder to leave, but I have also come to understand a much more powerful and primitive force that can keep us in relationships that we know, at some level, we should no longer be in. Without going into too much detail,

DOI: 10.4324/9781003172734-2

scientists now think we have three brains that have evolved into one over time.

BRAIN ONE: REPTILIAN BRAIN

Millions of years ago, the first brain to evolve was what has since been named the 'reptilian brain'. The reptilian brain manages all our basic, vital survival responses, such as breathing, keeping our organs functioning, regulating our temperature – are we too hot or too cold etc. – and the need to reproduce to keep our species going. The main part of the reptilian brain is there to ignite our fight, flight or freeze response to maintain survival. This is relevant to help us understand that, underneath all our thinking, the brain is constantly trying to determine whether or not we are safe. The first thing we do when we walk into a room is look around to see who is in it. Unconsciously we are trying to ascertain our safety as well as ascertain whether there is a social group that we can join. It is our reptilian brain's job to make sure we survive, so it is this part of our brain that has a powerful drive to keep us alive.

BRAIN TWO: MAMMALIAN BRAIN

The second brain that evolved to surround the reptilian brain is what is termed the mammalian brain. This is the part that creates and processes emotions and feelings towards others and, as mammals (animals and humans), to our young. The mammalian brain recognises that being in social groups and being connected with others is safer for our survival. For example, if you are an antelope in a herd, it is safer for you to be part of the herd rather than pushed outside of it. If you are pushed outside, you are more likely to get eaten by a lion or other predator. This could be the reason why some human beings have such a strong ignition of 'survival thinking' when rejected from a social group, relationship or partnership, with a feeling of panic if the relationship is breaking down. Metaphorically we are being pushed outside the social group. This unconsciously triggers the mammalian brain into believing we are not safe. Our brain could think that we are at risk of being exposed to prey and, subsequently, of dying. While this is not true in modern society, the primitive part of the brain still feels the need to alert us to the possibility. It is likely that this very strong survival response is activated when we split up with a close partner. This situation can make us feel extremely vulnerable and could explain why we believe we feel safer with a partner that is not good for us, rather than without them. Imagine if your brain actually thought you were at risk of dying if you were left on your own. The strong pull to remain in an unhealthy relationship would likely win out. Even when we are in a bad relationship, it offers us protection from being alone and therefore it feels safer to stay. If we can recognise that the strong feelings of vulnerability may be underpinned by a survival response, it could help us make the decision that it would be healthier for us to leave. If you are reading this then the hope is that you are already in a safe place and no longer in an unhealthy relationship.

BRAIN THREE: THINKING BRAIN (PRE-FRONTAL CORTEX)

The third part of our brain to develop was the extraordinary ability we have as human beings to be able to observe our own thinking and look inwards at our own thoughts. You may notice that a prey animal such as a zebra or antelope will react instantly if it senses danger and run away. As soon as the danger has passed it will put its head down to eat again. If it had the ability to predict it may never come back out to eat, too scared that a lion could still be nearby. Unlike animals, human beings have gone on to develop the ability to predict and have rational thought to help keep us safe, for example: 'that lion may still be out there'. The thinking brain (pre-frontal cortex) can also think rationally over and above the emotional response. 'There is no lion and, if there was, it would now be 20 miles away because I got into my car and drove off.' This allows us to think things through, problem solve and view different perspectives logically. With this unique ability to observe our own emotion, we are offered the opportunity to heal from emotional damage (Curran, 2008).

We have such a strong built-in sense of survival that our brains are wired to remember and learn from experience, and then alert us instantly if it is felt we could be at risk. This is a positive in terms of our survival, but it can also be a negative when it comes to trying new things or trusting people again. Our ability to predict can also create many anxious feelings and thoughts that are not helpful to us and keep us stuck.

It is possible that if you have been in a relationship of mistrust, you could develop insecurities. These may include areas such as a lack of confidence in yourself, your looks and a general struggle to trust people. If we are not aware of our thinking, it is very easy for our reptilian and mammalian brains to alert us to perceived danger that we feel we should act on, before really thinking if it is relevant in the here and now.

With this knowledge, we can start to make better decisions and choose healthier responses by using our 'thinking brain'. We can examine if we are just reacting from a place of survival and then make a better choice. Figure 2.1 shows that,

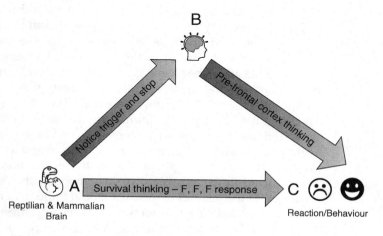

Figure 2.1: Brain training model

initially, when A) our reptilian and mammalian brains alert us to help us survive, we could respond with a fight, flight or freeze response and go straight to C) a place of an automatic reaction or behaviour. With knowledge of our thoughts, however, we can feel the alert from A) and then engage our thinking brain B) to see if there is a better choice and whether we really are under threat or not. We can then either choose a more helpful reaction or behaviour C).

The aim is to start to train your brain to go from A) to B) to C) rather than from A) straight to C).

Case study

Jodie was 32 years old. She had been in a difficult relationship for 3 years when she found out that her partner had recently been unfaithful to her. All her fears came to be realised, which created a huge amount of pain and anxiety for her. The relationship ended, leaving Jodie feeling very insecure as well as lowering her confidence and self-esteem. Eventually, Jodie did find another partner who loved and respected her, but although she was in a very safe and loving relationship, the feeling of insecurity was hard for her to manage. If Jodie did not do something about these feelings, this was likely to cause problems in the new relationship.

Jodie's insecurity was a natural response from both her reptilian and mammalian brains, which were trying to protect her from further pain or from being left alone outside of her social group. These parts of her brain were flagging up an alert that her safety may be compromised, based on previous experience. A situation that could trigger this immediate response could be as simple as her witnessing her new partner laughing with someone she did not know or maybe hearing a text arrive on her partner's phone. Normally Jodie would have reacted by being distant or in a mood with her partner, and the feelings of mistrust would build in her.

Jodie's original reaction would be to respond from her reptilian/mammalian brain, A), to create a reaction/

---

behaviour, C). When Jodie understood that both parts of her brain would instantly jump to survival thinking of a fight, flight or freeze response, she was able to stop and develop her thinking brain (pre-frontal cortex) by reflecting on all the possibilities.

Using the model (Figure 2.1) she could now choose to go from A) to B), asking herself 'Is my reaction relevant to the here and now? Am I really under threat? Do I have any evidence for the way I am feeling? Is the alert from my brain just trying to keep me safe or is the feeling relevant to now?'.

The response Jodie chose from her thinking brain, B) to C), was to share her vulnerability with her new partner calmly and logically. With her partner's help and trust she was able to get past this feeling. With time and the right support, Jodie learned to trust again, and to question her thinking more readily. Conscious thinking can help us to avoid old patterns that are no longer helpful to us.

We have much more control over the way our brains operate than we realise. We can use our thoughts, within reason, to create positive change when we know how to do so. Our brains are powerful tools. They can help support us in our journey or work against us if we are unaware of how they work. We cannot always control the thoughts that we have, but we do have a choice of how we manage them when they arrive. Just because we think 'it', it does not mean it is true.

However, our current reality is probably based on the thought processes that we have used historically. There has been research into how our thoughts can be used deliberately to create the things we need and want (Church, 2018). Based on the premise that if we can create realities in our lives by focusing on them and thinking about them first, then it makes sense to be careful about what we think about most. In simple terms, what we think about most will be more likely to materialise. This is such a powerful piece of knowledge, however, there is a lot of middle ground and it doesn't necessarily mean if you think about becoming the Queen for long enough it will happen! However, it does mean that it is important to know that you can influence your reality with your thinking.

What we are today comes from our thoughts of yesterday, and our present thoughts build our life of tomorrow. Our life is the creation of our mind.

(Mascaro, 1973)

What I have learned is our subconscious (the largest part of our brain, which keeps us functioning, stores memories and so on) is constantly working to achieve what we are telling it. When we truly understand this, we can really begin to change our lives. Our brain does not care whether we focus on a positive or negative thought, it will just get on with the job of thinking about it. When we think things repeatedly, we are embedding this thought process into our brain and bringing energy to it. This makes it feel truer for us. We are creating a neural pathway in our subconscious. When we can understand how we think and what we need to know to help us think differently, we can then start to change our reality to a better one. One way of thinking about this is to imagine you are in a jungle on a well-worn path. If this path is walked every day, it is easy to use. The ground stays flat and the plants are kept back. The more you walk on it the more worn and accessible it becomes and the easier it is to walk along without any effort. In the same way, when you continually think the same thoughts the neural pathways in your brain become the paths of least resistance for those types of thoughts to flow. This makes it easy for the brain to keep thinking the same flow of thoughts, which if negative, are not helpful to us. When we know this, we can start to put the effort in to change our thinking to more helpful thoughts. When we start to change our thoughts to create new neural pathways, it is at first difficult and takes effort and commitment. It is like coming to the edge of the jungle where a path does not yet exist. It takes time to hack away at the undergrowth and make an in-road. But if you keep coming back to the same place every day and hacking a bit more and start to walk the new path, it will eventually become easy and accessible. In the same way, if you keep thinking a new helpful thought it will eventually become a new way of thinking.

Have you ever really wanted something to the point that all you do is think about it until you get it? Sometimes we are driven to buy things and we keep thinking about them until we gain them. Advertisers adopt this approach in that if they keep showing our brains an item while telling us that we need it, we will be more likely to be influenced into buying it. Many successful sports people adopt this determination of thought and visualise their end goal to make it more realistic in their mind. This is an illustration of the power of our thinking energy being channelled in a direction until we achieve what we think we want. Suffice to say, dedicated thinking towards one thing creates an energy enabling it to happen more easily than if you don't put effort into thinking about it at all.

If we are intent on thinking a thought, whether positive or negative, our brain will do its best to create it for us. This, in turn, fuels our beliefs and can become a self-fulfilling prophecy.

There is a saying that the definition of insanity is to keep doing the same thing and expecting different results. If we keep doing what we have always done, we will keep getting what we have always got. You cannot expect to create different results in your life unless you are committed to changing your thinking.

Our brains also find it hard to process a negative. For example, if I say, 'don't think of a pink elephant', in order not to think about it, our brains must first think about it. Therefore, when we start to set more helpful outcomes for ourselves, they must be set in the positive and the present. For example, 'I am a great cook' rather than 'I don't cook badly'. From this sentence our brain would interpret 'cook badly' and we would be more likely to get those results. This may seem trivial, but understanding that our brain can work in often simplistic ways can help us to train our brains more effectively. Being careful and more accurate with our thoughts and language can help steer us to better results. There is more on goal setting in Step 9.

HOW DO WE DO THIS?

The first stage is to identify the beliefs and values that are important to you, as they will influence and underpin your thinking. But before we explore beliefs and values (Step 4 and Step 5), it will be helpful to understand how these all work together.

One school of thought is that our thoughts create our feelings, which create our behaviours. Another school of thought is that our feelings create our thoughts, which create our behaviours. Whichever way round will be personal to you, but for arguments sake, let us work with the first one.

Thoughts = Feelings = Behaviours

If this is the case, to create a different reality we need to review the thoughts we have, to create different feelings, which will make us behave differently, helping to create more helpful behaviours. When your behaviour starts to change in positive ways you naturally get different responses from others, which begin to create a different reality. We then have a different reality and future. I know this may look easy on paper, but it takes a lot of brain energy, which is why people find it difficult to change. It is easier to fall back into old, well-established ways of thinking.

Be aware of the thoughts you are having but recognise they are just thoughts until you act on them. My thoughts were I was fat, ugly and stupid. While I thought it, I believed it, and that was what I saw in the mirror and how others treated me. I then started to challenge those thoughts when they came up with, 'Who says?' 'What evidence do I really have that this is true?' 'What evidence do I have contrary to that?' 'What would a better thought be for me today?' 'How do I want to be seen?" More about this in Step 6 on how to build confidence.

We need to revisit our path in the jungle analogy and remember the description of the route of least resistance. At first it is difficult, as we need to struggle to tread down plants and move foliage aside. We could easily give up and go back to the old path (old way of thinking), which is the path of least resistance. However, if we keep on persistently going back to the new place and keep treading it down, we will create a new path (new positive thoughts) and it will eventually get easier and take us to a new destination. In other words, our new way of thinking will just become part of who we are. This is what we desperately need after a bad relationship. We do not want to go back to the same thing. So, to create a different experience, we must do something differently. The hard bit is accepting that this will take emotional and mental effort, which is why you need to be in a state of recovery to do this. You need to have the energy to notice and re-direct your normal thought patterns into a different thought process. You will be unable to make mental and emotional changes when you are still in the emotional place of a flight, fight, freeze response. To create something differently we need to do something differently. Small changes to your thinking every day will add up to powerful changes in your life!

 THINK FOR A MOMENT

Why do you believe a negative thought without evidence but not a positive one? If you are prepared to believe a negative one, then you should equally be prepared to believe a positive one.

In summary, we must learn to focus on positive, not negative, thoughts and give our brains some direction for our own good. It is important to think about and concentrate on the things that we *do* want, not what we *do not* want. Many people when asked tell us that they naturally think about what they *don't* want 80 per cent of the time, using up their energy unwisely in this task.

EXAMINE YOUR THOUGHTS

How often are you thinking of what you would like rather than what you *do not* want? Be conscious and observant of your thoughts and notice how often you are thinking negatively about yourself, others or a situation. You could keep a chart using the bar gate method and draw a line every time you notice, then change the thought to a more positive one. If you catch yourself thinking about what you *do not* want, then change your thoughts to focus on what you *do* want.

While we have hundreds and thousands of thoughts a day, it will start to show you how often you are thinking in a way that is no longer helpful to you. One of my clients recently asked what my observation was on how well people succeeded in change in relation to their thinking. After reflecting, my observation is that people's thoughts are sometimes more heavily weighted to being in either the past, or the present and future. For those that I have worked with whose thoughts are in the past, they appear more likely to suffer from feelings of depression. Those that can re-focus their thoughts on the present and future become more positive and hopeful, although I do not have any evidence to base this on other than observation.

 WHERE DOES MOST OF YOUR THINKING TAKE PLACE?

In the past, present or future? And where do you need to start focusing on?

The power of language

INTRODUCTION

This Step explores the power of language and the potential positive or negative impact that it can have on your daily life. It shows the power that words hold when they are used consistently and illustrates the effect they can have. It offers insights into how substituting more helpful words can reduce feelings of overwhelm and create a more positive reality than previously imagined. Changing your language can change your world!

Why is language so important? Basically, it carries meaning and is a way of communication, even to ourselves. Changing your language can change your reality, from one of feeling overwhelmed to one of potential balance. It is worth becoming aware of the way you speak to yourself and others and the type of language you use. What type of things do you say? Do you generalise a lot? Do you say things like, 'they always do that' or 'everyone thinks that way', or even, 'I always do that?' Stop and think: who is 'they', who is 'everyone'? What do they always do? Has it only happened once or twice? These generalisations can start to affect our mood by giving our brain the impression that things are insurmountable, hopeless or much worse than they really are. Recognising when we are generalising or making assumptions in a negative way and challenging those thoughts can help make our current reality better. There is an expression called 'clean language'. When I first heard this, I thought it meant not swearing! What it really means though is keeping the words that you are saying as clear and factual as possible. Many coaches are trained to use 'clean' language, as they do not want to create feelings

DOI: 10.4324/9781003172734-3

or thoughts within their coachee that were not already there, or assume they know what their coachee is thinking or feeling.

Case study

Debbie had quite a stressful life after becoming a single working parent with two children under 10 years old. She would use her humour to make light of her deeper feelings in order to be entertaining and funny when describing it to others. Her humour was based on negative descriptions of how her life felt. She had quite a few stock phrases that would make others laugh when she was describing her life, including saying things like, "it's like having your hands tied behind your back whilst trying to row a boat" and "people just suck the life out of me" etc.

Whilst for Debbie this is how her reality felt, when we explored the concept of how our thoughts create our feelings, she started to realise that the language she was using daily was creating feelings inside her that were unnecessarily negative.

Her phrases were momentarily funny for others but the continual use of them had a negative impact on how she was feeling on a day-to-day basis. There is no doubt that Debbie was in a tough situation, but when she stopped using her negative phrases and kept her language based on fact, her feelings of overwhelm and helplessness began to reduce. This reduction in the negative feelings that she had previously felt weighed down by, just by changing her language, meant that she instead felt able to cope with her situation. Debbie continued to use happier phrases about her life.

 TAKE NOTE OF YOUR LANGUAGE

Do you tend to generalise in a negative way? If so, try to turn it around. Be aware of the sort of things you are generalising or exaggerating and try to replace those words with the facts of the situation. For example: 'I have hundreds of things to do', change with, 'I have one, two or three, things to do' – however many there are.

This can help you gain a new perspective and relieve feelings of being overwhelmed, enabling you to see things as being manageable.

Writing things down also helps in getting thoughts outside of our head, enabling us to gain a realistic viewpoint. It can free up space for better thinking, rather than everything being jumbled up inside your head. This can help you become focused and gain perspective on whether things are really that bad or whether your brain is exaggerating. The journaling tool is useful here.

BREAK THINGS DOWN

If you are feeling overwhelmed by the number of things you must do, then break them down into areas that can be done together and those that are individual tasks. We often say we have not got enough time, but if we break jobs down into bite-size pieces and accurate completion times, we can quickly see that things are not as bad as we first thought.

THE 10-MINUTE RULE

Assign yourself 10 minutes for any outstanding task and then stop. If the ironing pile is too high or the paperwork has not been done, just decide to do 10 minutes. This will soon make in-roads into things that appear too big to tackle. It also means that small daily efforts will eventually get the job done without overwhelming you.

STEP 4
Understanding your values

INTRODUCTION

This Step explains what is meant by values and how they are the drivers to a person's behaviours, happiness and motivation. It includes an exercise that helps you identify your own values, which can become a guiding compass for any future decision making.

All of us have a subconscious hard drive in our brain running the day-to-day functioning of everything we do, just like the operating system behind the scenes on your computer. We do not often think about this, but most of our decision making and opinions will arrive from two areas inside our heads. The first is our values. These are the mental and emotional standards we hold about what we consider to be important or unimportant for ourselves and others in our lives. The second is our belief system. This is what we have been led to believe, by others or ourselves, in terms of what we think to be true about ourselves and the world. I will explore both in more detail, as they underpin our thinking and decision making. It could be that you have never thought about them, and yet they are the silent program running in the background, guiding the everyday choices that create your life.

WHAT ARE THEY AND WHY ARE THEY SO IMPORTANT?

Our behaviour is often based on our values. Our values create our behaviour, not the other way around. When we are living our lives in line with our values, we are more likely to be successful, happy, content and productive. I have often

 DOI: 10.4324/9781003172734-4

coached people who are in their 40s and slowly come to realise they are very unhappy in their work. They find they are working in a job their parents wanted them to do and had never stopped to think that it may not be important to them. It is only with this recognition that they can then discover what is significant to them and will make them happy, before they can move on to a brighter future. By not identifying our values we can be left feeling like a square peg in a round hole, that we do not 'fit' or we are unhappy but cannot work out why.

Values are an expression of ourselves. Values can differ immensely from person to person and, at worst, our partner could hold totally opposing values to our own. This often happens in relationships without any knowledge or intention and can be a trigger for conflict, especially if you are in a difficult relationship. It is important to recognise that everybody has a slightly different value base, and what is important to you may not be as important to another person. Knowing this can help maintain respect for other people's values when they are different to yours, which can help avoid or reduce conflict. I have learned that knowing my values is a hugely important and worthwhile exercise. Since recognising what my values are, all my decision making has been measured against these so I can consciously make a decision that works for me. Once you have identified the values that are most important to you, you can use these as a foundation to support any future decision making, like having your own internal guiding compass to happiness.

If you find it difficult to identify your values, it may be helpful to think about the things that make you upset or angry. It can be that if someone is acting in a way that is opposed to your values, you may find it distressing, uncomfortable or feel annoyed. For example: if one of your values is honesty and you have a partner that keeps lying to you, you would find this very difficult to deal with. Our behaviour and choices are underpinned by our values, whether we are conscious of them or not. Decisions made from your value base will be more likely to be in line with your own authenticity, helping to create a more rewarding and congruent reality.

Case study

Karen was 25 years old. She had lived with her partner for 8 years and they didn't have any children. She was a very generous character and tried hard to make the relationship work, often by putting her own needs on hold to please her partner. Sadly, the relationship had broken down as she felt she could never get anything right. She was struggling to make decisions about her future and she needed to find somewhere to live. She was also trying to understand why her relationship had proved to be so difficult and described it as 'always feeling such hard work'. When the relationship ended, she wanted to move on with her life but felt she needed to reflect and understand what had happened, and why, so that she didn't make a similar mistake again.

When Karen went through the values exercise, she started to gain clarity about what was important to her as an individual. She had never thought explicitly about what really mattered to her, and quickly recognised that her previous partner's values would have been completely different to her own. This helped Karen realise that it was not that she was right or wrong but that it was deep, personal differences that had created the difficult relationship for her.

Once she had identified her top 10 personal and important values, she was able to use them to support her decision making when finding a new home. Karen could make sure that she had somewhere with a garden, as nature was important to her. She knew that when she met another person, if they had similar values to herself, then she would more likely feel at ease with them.

 THINK ABOUT THE THINGS THAT REALLY MATTER TO YOU

Figure 4.1 gives some examples of values. Circle the ones that you feel are most important to you. Use any spare space to add any that are not already included.

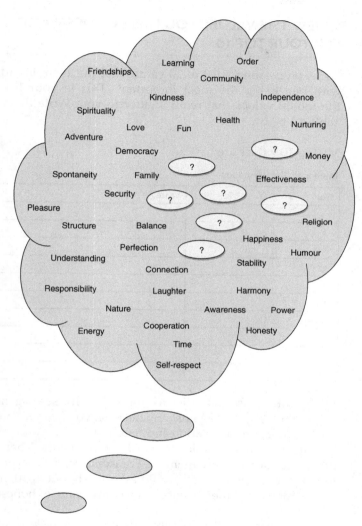

Figure 4.1: Brain of values

REVIEW THE VALUES YOU HAVE CHOSEN AND PICK YOUR TOP 10

Focus on creating a list of 10 values and put them in order, with one being the most important. This is your list of the top 10 values that really matter to you. Write them in Table 4.1 below.

My top 10 values are:

Table 4.1: Top 10 values

No:	Value
1	
2	
3	
4	
5	
6	
7	
8	
9	
10	

In the future use your list to guide you by scoring how happy you might be against any decision you need to make, for example, work/relationship/job and so on. To do this, imagine each value holds a worth of 10 points. Then go down the list and score them all. For example, if I was going to move to a new house, I would ask myself, out of 10, how would moving to the new house meet my value of honesty?

'I am being honest with myself about what I need and where I want to live so, yes, it would probably be an eight.' Then put eight in the box next to 'honesty'.

Next ask yourself how well moving to your new house would meet your value of family.

'*It would be a great new home and much better for my family so would score a 10.*' Then put a 10 in the box next to family. Continue down the list until each of your values have been scored against your new decision. When each box has a score, add them up to get the total.

How well does the new decision meet your values? The higher the score (if 10 is the best), the happier and more successful you are likely to be. For example, if I were scoring 70 out of 100 in terms of my values being met in the new scenario I would very likely be happy. However, if I was only scoring 40 it may be worth re-evaluating the decision.

Table 4.2: Decision-making grid

No:	Value	New decision (for example: moving to a new house I have seen)	Thoughts
1	Honesty	8	
2	Family	10	
3	Love	7	
4	Freedom	9	
5	Friendships	7	
6	Nature	5	
7	Creativity	2	
8	Challenge	6	
9	Learning	4	
10	Serenity	8	
	Total score out of 100	66	

Once you are clear about your values you can use them as your guiding compass in life. When you need to make future decisions about your career, job, role, relationships, etc., you can score them out of 10 against your values, in terms of satisfaction, and see how well the decision will suit who you are as a person. This will ultimately impact on how happy and satisfied you are likely to be because of the choices you are about to make. You can also have fun and get a potential new partner to do the exercise so that you can both see what is important to you individually. Making decisions based on your values will mean decision making more closely aligns to what you really want and who you are.

 ## HONOUR YOUR VALUES

Think about what sort of things you need to have in your life to honour your values and write some examples down here. It could be finding friends with similar values. It could be making time to go for a walk in the countryside if you value nature or go for a swim if you value fitness. What could you do to meet a value of creativity if you have one? In terms of any kind of relationship, the more the other person holds the same values as yourself, the happier the relationship is likely to be. Or at least your differences can be acknowledged and respected. This is important when you get to the stage of finding a supportive and respectful partner.

Re-assessing your beliefs

INTRODUCTION

This Step describes the power of your belief system and how it operates in the subconscious. It explains what beliefs are, why you need to know about them and how to identify them. There is an exercise to determine your own positive and negative beliefs, which offers the opportunity to create more beneficial beliefs, and so create a preferred reality.

We all have beliefs. Some of them are helpful to us and some of them are unhelpful. The power of our belief system must not be underestimated and will be impacting on our daily lives and our future. The Cambridge Dictionary definition of belief is 'the feeling of being certain that something exists or is true' (*Cambridge Online Dictionary*, n.d.). It is basically a principle that is accepted as true or real without proof – an opinion, a conviction.

The beliefs we hold are thoughts that are no longer questioned. They are usually held so deeply that they operate seamlessly in the background of our minds, without us even realising they are there. They have the power to create and destroy our lives because the decisions we make will be based on these beliefs. Therefore, it is important to be clear about the beliefs you hold about yourself and the world around you, and where they came from.

Our beliefs are usually formed in early childhood and teenage years when we are trying to make sense of the world. Often our beliefs about relationships are also formed at this early stage from witnessing how our parents relate to each other. This creates a blueprint in our mind of what is

DOI: 10.4324/9781003172734-5

a 'normal' relationship. Beliefs can be influenced by people, such as parents, relatives, guardians and teachers, and other sources, such as news outlets. One example of a belief system is religion. I realised that religious views were formed in my life by other people's opinions before I was able to look at them more objectively for myself as an adult. Once I could recognise them as beliefs, I could then make a choice as to whether they were helpful to me or not, and if I wanted to keep them or choose different ones. It helped me understand why others thought and acted the way they did. I was able to witness the evidence of good and bad behaviour that humans exhibit based on their beliefs. We must not underestimate the power of beliefs.

If we received positive, loving and encouraging messages from our parents, relatives, teachers and others, we would more likely have healthy beliefs about ourselves. However, if we were heavily criticised, ridiculed, blamed and shouted at, we are very likely to carry some negative beliefs about ourselves.

It has been recognised that as parents we often give small children 10 negative comments to every positive comment. It is for that reason that verbal abuse is more widely recognised as a significant issue for children. I noticed when my children were young that I was speaking to other people's children far more respectfully than my own. This awareness then allowed me to speak more respectfully to my children. The more I tried to speak from my adult and nurturing parent place, the better response I gained from my children. I was able to model how I would like them to communicate and behave while allowing them to express their emotions, as they were not yet able to articulate them in an adult way. I could change my beliefs given to me about parenting.

Whatever messages we were given by those around us in childhood, we often believe them to be true about ourselves. They become such a deeply embedded part of who we 'think' we are. They also inform how we feel we fit into and make sense of the world. We no longer question them and continue to take them into adulthood.

Case study

Kevin was 34 years old, very generous and kind by nature, and always tried to please his partner. The relationship had deteriorated after the first couple of years, with his wife behaving very disrespect-fully towards him a lot of the time. She would put him down in front of others and criticise his actions constantly. Whatever Kevin did wasn't good enough. Kevin's 'try harder' nature had kept him in the rela-tionship, thinking that if he could just be better and get things right then she would be happy. He had invested a great deal of himself in making sure his partner's needs were met, both emotionally and financially, as far as he could. He rarely put himself first as he believed this was selfish behaviour. Due to his wife's disapproval, he had very few close friends outside the relationship and she actively dissuaded him from going out on his own and meeting others. When things finally broke down after 10 years, Kevin was left without friends, hobbies or interests to support him through this difficult time.

When Kevin reflected and understood his beliefs, he realised that he had looked after his partner at the expense of his own needs and done nothing much for himself for many years. He had previously believed that doing nice things for himself was selfish. This belief had originated from his childhood when he had wanted to do his own thing as a child but had brothers and sisters who didn't have the same interests. He reviewed his beliefs around his own importance and decided that looking after himself was not being selfish, and he could still look after others as well. He started to re-connect with friends that he had lost touch with and joined a running group. He incorporated his joy of running to make himself happy with raising money for charity. This served both his new belief of looking after himself with the belief that helping others was important. It also provided him with an additional sense of purpose.

Creating a new belief can help to create a better reality, but it does take time and commitment to change your thinking in this area. If you get in your car and drive the same route every day you will end up in the same place. If you make a small adjustment by turning your steering wheel 2 centimetres to the right, for a while your journey will appear to be the same, but as time goes on you will end up at a totally different destination. By making small changes in your thinking, you will, in time, gain a new reality. The good news is that, as an adult with a new-found awareness, you can make a choice over the beliefs you hold. When you believe something, your brain helps you to find evidence that it is true. This, in turn, supports your belief, reinforcing it. You will find more evidence because you believe it and so on. When you can recognise a belief is no longer valid or useful to you, you can go about changing it. The trick is to recognise that this takes time and, while you can commit to change the 'belief' overnight, the reality is set in a time lag. The hard part is that you must begin thinking of the new belief as true before it becomes true – then, slowly, you will begin to find new evidence to support it. This is where your commitment to yourself comes in.

For example, one person may believe the world is a scary place. Because of this belief their brain is more likely to detect and pick up on things that may be more worrying or frightening from the television and news that they are exposed to. Their brain is trying to keep them alert to remain safe. The brain will create a focus on the negative information available, which in turn will confirm their belief to be true.

Another person may believe the world is an exciting place, full of opportunity, love and freedom. They will equally find evidence to support this. Individually, we all have a different reality that has been made up of our experiences, belief systems and filters.

The important thing now is to review your beliefs and clear out any that are destructive for you or have trapped you in a destructive place.

FILL IN THE STARS

Fill each star in Figure 5.1 with a positive belief you have about yourself, for example: 'I am kind'.

Now fill each thought cloud in Figure 5.2 with a negative belief you have about yourself, for example: 'I am bad at relationships'.

Which was easier? Most of us find it difficult to think of positive beliefs about ourselves. I am hoping that even if it was difficult, you will have found at least one positive belief. The very fact that you are starting this journey and this workbook is proof that you believe you are worth making the effort for.

Figure 5.1: Positive belief stars

Figure 5.2: Negative belief clouds

Figure 5.3: New belief banner

I believe you absolutely are and, in my experience, this is the perfect start to a new and fulfilling life!

It is worth exploring each negative and positive belief to help understand where you think it came from and if you need to re-assess it.

 ASK YOURSELF

Ask yourself: 'From the beliefs I have identified can I recall where or who they may have come from? Was it from a parent or grandparent and did I hold them in high regard? What do I think of them now and would I still trust their opinion? Is this a helpful belief for me going forwards in my life? If not, how might it affect the rest of my life if I keep believing this? If I could replace this for a different, more helpful belief, how might my life change in a positive way?'

 A NEW BELIEF

Think of a new belief that could begin to help you in your life. Make it something that you believe is possible for you one day. Write it down in the new belief banner (Figure 5.3), then review the other beliefs you have and do the same. Start to challenge your old, unhelpful beliefs as you become aware that you are thinking them.

Building confidence

INTRODUCTION

This Step helps you to explore and focus on what confidence means for you.

It highlights the importance of understanding how your inner voice can be damaging to your confidence and explains why it is important to become your own best friend. Confidence-building tools are offered.

Confidence is a word we all use and most of us would like more of it. However, it can be difficult to pin down what we mean by confidence. I spent around 30 years of my life apologising to everyone that I met with an 'I'm sorry' at the start of many of my sentences. I was not confident enough to just state what I thought. I know it can be hard to state what your needs are or to have an opinion out of fear of rejection or for some other reason. It is worth thinking about the following.

WHAT DOES CONFIDENCE MEAN FOR YOU?

Take a moment and note down what it means for you personally.

DOI: 10.4324/9781003172734-6

If you do not think you have any confidence, then think about the things you do have confidence in, such as the fact that the weather will change or summer will come after spring. At some level you will have some confidence in something. Confidence is like a muscle and over time it can build and grow, but just like a muscle you need to start exercising it slowly and in small steps. Eventually you will become more confident.

 HAVE A LOOK AT THE LIST BELOW AND ANSWER THE QUESTIONS

- How is a lack of confidence affecting you?

- What will you be doing when you are more confident?

- What will you look like?

- What sort of things will you hear yourself saying?

- How will you be feeling differently?

WHAT YOU CAN DO TO HELP YOU FEEL MORE CONFIDENT

- Note down when you have a success and be proud of yourself even if they are small achievements.
- Choose a more positive belief that can help your confidence and practise it until it feels natural for you.

- Hang out with people that can support you and make you feel good and spend less time with those that don't.
- Be aware that your inner voice is not critical towards yourself. If you realise you are being more unkind to yourself than you would ever dream of being to your best friend, then stop and be kinder. Saying negative things to yourself will constantly undermine your own confidence.
- Focus on what you do want. Have awareness on where your thoughts are going and redirect your thinking back to what you do want and away from what you don't want!
- Forgive yourself when things go wrong, as we can only learn by making mistakes.
- Visualisations – see yourself being more confident in your mind. Practise every evening before sleeping. Close your eyes and really see yourself being confident and happy. What are you wearing, is it day or night, what can you hear people saying about you, what can you smell and feel? Make it as real as possible in your mind.
- Strategies – what can you practise? Take small steps. If things do not go as well as hoped then remind yourself of what you are good at.
- Are you comparing yourself to others? I was once given a good bit of advice that if I was going to compare myself to someone, then make sure they were much worse than me. The point being that we are prepared to take a negative view of our ability as true but not a positive one.

Don't compare yourself to others as you are unique.

ENCOURAGE YOURSELF

What qualities do you have? If you have been in an abusive relationship, stamina is a quality many people have. Patience and empathy are also common. Think hard to find your qualities – they will be there. If you really do not know, ask a few friends or colleagues to write down what they think (this can be done anonymously) and feed back to you.

MAKE A NOTE OF THE THINGS YOU ARE GOOD AT

Remind yourself as you go through the day what qualities you are showing. At the end of the day review this. It may have been just the will to get through the day – that is a quality in itself.

So far you have survived 100% of your worst days – you're doing great!

(livehappy.com, 2020)

PRACTISE FORGIVENESS

Forgiveness may not be high on your agenda after what you have experienced. However, honing the art of forgiveness is crucial, purely to allow yourself to move on. I do not see it as letting others 'off the hook'. I see it in a more selfish way – if I can forgive, it will help me to move on and not keep me stuck in a negative place. The other person may never know that I have forgiven them. Practise forgiving yourself and others. Attaching blame either to yourself or anyone else is a negative habit that won't help you. This will help you to overcome obstacles more quickly and not drain your energy.

Forgiving ourselves can be one of the hardest things to do

A CONFIDENCE NOTEBOOK

Get yourself a confidence notebook and write down the times in your life when you tried something new. Whether you succeeded or failed is irrelevant, the fact that you had the confidence to try it is what matters. Confidence is about having the ability to act without worrying about what you are unable to do and still having the courage to have a go.

READ YOUR LIST

At the end of the week read your list back to yourself aloud. It is nice to put on your favourite music when you do this as it can be really uplifting. It creates a positive anchor of good feelings. If you keep practising this there will come a time when you only need to play the music to start to feel good and be much more confident.

We often know of someone who we think of as confident and wish we could be more like them. You can do a visualisation exercise in which you request to borrow their confidence.

CIRCLE OF CONFIDENCE EXERCISE

Get nice and relaxed in a quiet place where you will not be disturbed. Put some soothing music on quietly if you want to. With your eyes closed, imagine taking an expanding circle of light out of your pocket and then place it on the floor in front of you. This will be big enough for you to visualise yourself stepping into later. Imagine a confident person that you rate, standing in front of you in the circle of light. What are they wearing, how are they standing, what is their body language like, what makes them confident? What is their tone of voice and what type of words do they use? Really get a feel for this person. When you are ready, ask them (in your mind) if you can step into their body and take on their 'confident' qualities. They will obviously say yes. Still with your eyes closed, take a step forward into the circle and into their body (making sure you do not bang into anything). Really get a feel of what it is like to be them, to be confident. What is your body language now doing? What words will you be using and will you hear yourself saying? How will you be standing? When you have been fully immersed in the experience and it begins to subside, say 'thank you' and step back out of the circle. Then pick the circle up and put in your pocket. You can practise this exercise two or three times until you feel that you have really absorbed their qualities. Now, every time you need to feel a little more confident you can place your imaginary circle down on the floor and step into it to take on those positive characteristics!

Confidence is a perception, and many people appear to be more confident than they actually would say they are if you asked them. Acting *as if* you are confident automatically takes you to a place where people will see you as confident (even if you don't feel it). This will be reflected back to you and in turn increase your confidence!

BODY LANGUAGE

Just by changing your body language to be more upright with your shoulders back and having eye contact will make you look and feel more confident. I recommend reading the book *Confidence Booster Workout – 10 Steps to Beating Self Doubt* (Perry, 2004) for more on this.

PRACTISE CONFIDENCE

Write down here one thing you can do in the next week to practise being confident.

INNER VOICE

Internally, most of us have a little voice chatting to us throughout the day. Sometimes it is helpful and other times it is a real pain in the butt! What sort of little voice do you have? Is it a helpful, kind and supportive voice or a critical, humiliating voice? Is it your voice or one of your parents?

How we speak to ourselves internally will enormously affect our confidence. I expect your confidence may have taken a bit of a battering if you are reading this book. Imagine a child learning to walk. As a parent or adult, if you hold that little hand and encourage the child every time it falls over, using kind words and phrases, the child will enjoy learning to walk and gain a sense of achievement when they do well. If, however, you get cross with the child for tripping, falling over or being so stupid every time they make a mistake, then the child will feel sad, probably doubt their ability and want to give up. You need to treat your inner child with respect and kindness. To gain awareness of how you speak to yourself start to really listen to your inner voice.

 ## RECORD YOUR INNER VOICE

Keep a record over a week of how many times you have noticed you are unkind to yourself and what sort of things you have said.

I want you to listen to yourself and take note of what you say. If you have said something negative, then apologise to yourself and replace the negative statement with a kinder statement. Most people would not treat their friends or family with that level of disrespect, so you should not treat yourself like it. Begin to be your own best friend. When you make a mistake, forgive yourself. When you mess up or say the wrong thing, in your mind reassure yourself that you are doing your best. I cannot emphasise enough how important this is to help your inner confidence.

Be as kind to yourself as you would to your own best friend

STEP 7

Improving assertiveness

INTRODUCTION

This Step defines what assertiveness means and what you are entitled to and should expect in terms of assertiveness for yourself and others. A short case study demonstrates an example of how to build assertiveness to say 'no', amongst other examples of things to say and practise.

Being assertive is a skill that can be learned and improved upon. For me, this was one skill that I needed to work on as I would never put my own needs first. I felt it would be safer if I went along with everybody else. Being assertive felt like I was being opinionated, bossy or rude. If you have lost a lot of confidence and feel insecure, it is not easy to be assertive, especially if you have an ingrained response of trying to keep the peace by not having an opinion or preference for fear of upsetting someone else. If you are the sort of person who is always trying to please others, upsetting someone can be a terrifying prospect. It can feel amplified as you may worry the person may no longer be there for you or you will not be liked anymore. Feeling alone can create feelings of fear or of being abandoned – all these feelings can keep us stuck. While being abandoned may not be true, there is a part of your brain that is trying to look after you and may lead you to think this. I have had to learn to be assertive, and when I first set out on my journey it had not occurred to me that I had a right as a human being to request that I was treated in a certain way or that I had permission to act in a certain way. I have learned that good people won't leave me, get offended or love me any less if I am assertive. To the contrary, and to my surprise, I have found the opposite in that I am respected and my life will miraculously go on. So, please

DOI: 10.4324/9781003172734-7

practise a little bit of assertiveness, even if it is just deciding whether you want tea or coffee when someone asks you. You may relate to my response, which used to be, 'I don't mind', purely to make it easier for them! Assertiveness, confidence and self-esteem are all linked together and it is very difficult to be confident and assertive if your self-esteem is low. There are various ways that you can build your self-esteem and many books are available that focus on just that. When we have low self-esteem, we often feel that life's challenges are too hard for us to adequately sort out. We can carry a very low opinion of ourself, which undermines our confidence and wellbeing, and our feelings of being 'good enough'. If you feel you have or are suffering from low self-esteem, it may be helpful to get support through a qualified counsellor or therapist who can help provide you with some tools to develop this part of you.

ASSERTIVE RIGHTS

Assertiveness is all about the rights you have as an individual and being able to stand up for yourself in a calm and positive way. These are fair and balanced rights and can be expected by every human being. Assertiveness is neither being aggressive or passive in our communication but holding the middle ground. Being assertiveness is about respecting other opinions and, equally, having your opinions respected as well. Some assertiveness 'rights' that are recognised are given in Table 7.1.

Table 7.1: Assertiveness rights. This table helps to demonstrate the rights you and others have as a ground rule.

I	You
I have the right to be treated with respect as an equal human being.	Others have the right to be treated with respect as an equal human being.
I have the right to voice my own opinions and thoughts.	Others have the right to voice their opinions and thoughts.
I have the right to decide what is a priority for me regardless of other people's expectations or personalities.	Others have the right to decide what is a priority for them regardless of other people's expectations or personalities.

(continued)

Table 7.1 Cont.

I have the right to question things.	Others have the right to question things.
I have the right to express my feelings.	Others have the right to express their feelings.
I have the right to say no and not to feel guilty for doing so.	Others have the right to say no and not to feel guilty for doing so.
I have the right to say 'I don't understand'.	Others have the right to say 'I don't understand'.
I have the right to get things wrong and make mistakes.	Others have the right to get things wrong and make mistakes.
I have the right to change my mind.	Others have the right to change their minds.
I have the right to ask for what I want.	Others have the right to ask for what they want.
I have the right to not need other people's approval.	Others have the right to not need other people's approval.
I have the right to decide for myself whether I am responsible for finding a solution to another person's problem.	Others have the right to decide for themselves whether they are responsible for finding a solution to another person's problem.

You may notice that the table is based on things being equal for you and for someone else. To become more assertive, you will need to practise until you become comfortable being clear about your needs. Start by doing something small that is just out of your comfort zone. The example previously given about being clear whether you would like tea or coffee might be a great place to start. Listen to what you really want and make decisions based on that. This will help you get to a place where you are happier in yourself and you will start to notice you still have people around you who care but are much happier.

Another example could be, rather than saying, 'I think that is a really stupid idea', which would be perceived as aggressive, you could say something like, 'that is one idea but there may be others that might work as well'. A passive response could consist of no response at all, with you just accepting the opinions of others, even if you don't agree with them.

Case study

Brian was a middle-aged man working in an office environment as part of a team. He had recently divorced from his wife and subsequently saw less of his children. This meant he was in the office a little longer than those around him, as he no longer had to rush off to collect or drop off his children. Due to this, his manager often requested him to do things over and above what the rest of the team were asked to do. As Brian was not very assertive, he would always take on the extra work, but it started to leave him with feelings of resentment and frustration. Other people would have gone home while he felt he had to stay behind to meet the extra demands. Brian knew at some level that if he didn't learn to develop his assertive side, he would always end up feeling put out or undervalued. There was also a risk that he would end up moving and changing jobs as situations became too uncomfortable or difficult to manage. When Brian explored his fear of saying 'no' he realised it was due to the fear of not feeling needed or wanted, or losing favour or friendships. This was amplified due to his feelings of loss around his family unit.

Brian decided to find a way of saying 'no' that was comfortable to him and to practise this over the next few months. As a first step, rather than saying an outright 'no', he would suggest that if he took on this extra piece of work, he would need to let something else go and would ask the manager to prioritise which of the tasks he would prefer him to do. At first, he found it difficult to phrase it in a way that felt ok, but he soon realised that the more he did it, the easier it became. He was able to go home on time and let go of the feelings of resentment. He also began to feel a new sense of self-respect and respect from his team members and manager. Contrary to Brian's fears of losing friendships, he gained more respect and closer relationships because of being more assertive.

There are some ways you can practise assertiveness. One is being clear that what you are about to say is based on fact and is quite specific, rather than a generalisation such as, 'everybody wants this …'. An assertive approach based on facts would sound more like, 'there are two people who would like that option'. When what you are saying is based on fact it holds a strength of truth for you and you can feel stronger and more comfortable in what you are communicating. Another area where people find it difficult to be assertive is having the ability to say no. It can help to think of saying no as like building a weak, underdeveloped muscle. The more we practise the easier it will get, as it will become a natural response. However, to start, it can be difficult when we don't want to let people down or upset or offend anyone. So, rather than saying no, you could start to practise some phrases ready to respond when someone asks you to do something that you may not really want to do. For example, 'that's a very kind offer and I need to consider it properly before giving you my answer'. Or, 'I'm afraid I can't answer that now and need to check my diary/calendar or ask my partner'. Or, 'that's interesting, but I'm afraid I'm going to have to opt out this time as I have other engagements'. It is important not to tie yourself up in knots but try to buy yourself some time to find the right way of saying no. Often, telling the truth in a factual and kind way can be enough for people to understand, such as, 'that is such a kind offer, but sadly it will take up two hours of my day, which unfortunately I am unable to give at the moment'. So, think about a stock phrase that feels comfortable for you and start to use this when you are asked to do things that, in your heart, you know you should say no to.

When you are talking it is easy to slip into woolly words that are not really going to help you respect yourself, such as, 'I'll try' or 'It's only me' or 'I'll just do …'. Small words in your language such as 'try', 'only' and 'just' can start to demean your own power, so watch out for whether you are using these a lot in conversation and try to eliminate them.

Being assertive does not mean you will alienate yourself from others. It is useful though to note that there are always pros and cons to changing your behaviour. If people around you are very used to your old patterns, it can rock the boat when you start to change. People feel secure by certainty and predictability. When this changes it can sometimes give them a wobble. It helps to be aware of this as it may change how people initially experience you, but once they see the new, assertive you and understand the reasons for this new, consistent alignment of yourself, your relationships will settle back down and the people that are worth having around will still be around. You may want to share that you are practising being more assertive with the people closest to you so that they can support you.

 PRACTISE ASSERTIVENESS

Write down one new assertive action that you are going to practise.

 VISUALISE YOUR ASSERTIVENESS

Imagine that your assertiveness is developing in a way that is healthy for you and your relationships.

- How will you know it has developed?

- What will you notice about yourself?

- What will others notice about you?

- What will you be hearing, feeling and seeing when you are more assertive?

Designing your future

INTRODUCTION

This Step offers a fun and creative exercise to start to design your desired future. It offers step-by-step questions to support you in creating ideas of how you may want your life to be. The end product is a set of goals that are ready to be put into practice and that can be linked back to your personal wheel of life that you created in Step 1.

This is where things get exciting! I have come to realise that my thinking can either support me or bring me down. Your life ahead can be pretty much any way you choose it to be. That may sound glib but from my own experience of hitting rock bottom and losing nearly everything I had, I have now ultimately created a life I could only have imagined (and did!). For now, you do not need to be particularly realistic, so I would suggest you give yourself licence to dream big – the refining comes later. Planning your life is important and while these steps take time, they do work and are worth the effort. Many people spend longer planning a two-week holiday than their life, and often end up somewhere they do not want to be. So, have some fun with this part and allow yourself to be creative. At this stage you do not have to believe that your life can be how you want it to be, you just need to get started on some ideas. Ideas that excite you and raise your pulse. For some this may just be an end goal of peace and happiness. For others it may be an exciting adventure. This process can be tricky if your sense of self has been eroded, so take your time and begin to allow your mind to wander and really explore the thoughts that come up. If they are negative, recognise them and let them go, and redirect

DOI: 10.4324/9781003172734-8

your thinking to a positive thought and a positive vision – to something that makes you smile.

 ## HOW YOU WOULD LIKE YOUR LIFE TO BE?

Get a large piece of paper and some coloured pens (if you are feeling creative) and start to write down and draw pictures of all the things you would want in your future and how you would like your new future to be.

If you could wave a magic wand what would your future be like?

What hobbies would you like to do?	How would you like to be seen?
What sort of house would you like to live in?	Where would you like to live?
What job would you like to work in?	How would you want to dress?
What sort of friends would you like to have?	Would you like pets?

REVISIT THE LIST

The next day, reflect on your list and your drawings and start to revise it. Take away anything that doesn't really feel important to you and only leave the things that really matter to you in your life going forwards. Sometimes you will think of new things to add as once you have started to open your mind to possibilities lots of creative ideas can materialise.

WHY?

The next stage is to ask yourself the question, 'why are these things important to me?' Remember, we need to create things that are linked to our values if we want to be happy. For example, if you want to own an aviary but one of your values is 'freedom', seeing all the birds trapped or knowing you will have to be committed to feeding them every day may start to make you feel unhappy.

Review each item on your list, asking yourself what is important about it for you and why it would make a difference in your life. Make sure that everything that is left on your list is linked to your values. If you cannot find a good enough reason for it to be on your list, then get rid of the idea.

BACK TO THE WHEEL OF LIFE

You are now going to look back at the important areas from your earlier wheel of life. List your segments from the wheel.

1

2

3

4

5

6

7

8

Take a while to assess whether what you have identified on your list fits within the segments of your life. Are there any that do not fit? If so, do you need to add an additional segment to your wheel of life or is it not that important after all? Remember that the eight areas you choose on your wheel are completely your choice.

The next stage is to identify which segment from your wheel you want to work on first. Which is a priority? It does not have to be the lowest scoring segment – it is about which aspect of your life feels right for you to focus your attention on first.

Choose a segment and look at its current score. Think about what is giving it that score now. Next think about what it would have to be like to be a 10. What would be happening if this area was perfect?

If you were currently scoring three for satisfaction in this segment and you have identified what would make it a 10, then think about one small step that would move you towards that – a step that would incrementally move the satisfaction score one point higher in that area of your life. What could you do that is achievable and realistic to bring that score up by one?

 ONE SMALL STEP

Write down one small step that will improve the area you have chosen to focus on and that you can turn into a goal in the next step of this workbook.

THE STEP AND THE VALUES

Review how well the steps meet your values. What new belief may you need to help you? What resources will you need? (Support of a friend to hold you to account, for example.) How will you feel if it does not happen? How will you feel if it does happen?

You can then do the same process for each segment of your wheel. The next stage is to form these steps towards your future into tangible goals that you can achieve.

Setting goals

INTRODUCTION

This Step emphasises the importance of goal setting and why it is an effective method of achievement. It focuses on the different types of goals and why making them measurable is essential. It offers the GROW model as a tool for you to use to set realistic and small goals, and outlines when larger strategic goals can, and need, to be broken down into smaller steps. You can introduce the goals that you have created in the previous Steps and assess them against the GROW model and the wheel of life.

The tried and tested way of achieving things is to set targets or goals. These do not have to be enormous in the first instance. In fact, it is much better to set yourself small but realistic goals that can be easily achieved. This will help build your confidence and momentum. There is a great saying that if you do not make your own plans others will make them for you. By being clear about what it is that you want, you can begin to shape your life. Just like if you are in the ocean in a boat and want to get to a far-off island, you need to start holding the rudder of the boat to steer you in that general direction – even though the island may be miles away. As you come close to the island you can start to get more specific about how to land. It is said that a goal is like a dream but with a date. Without a timeframe and being specific about what it is that you do want, you are not likely to achieve it. There is now lots of research supporting the fact that people who set goals and write them down are far more likely to achieve what they set out to do.

Don't be disheartened when things don't happen overnight. The changes you are making today are creating a better

 DOI: 10.4324/9781003172734-9

future, but to achieve them, there is likely to be a time lag – just like sailing. If you have somewhere on the horizon that you want to sail to, but you don't bother keeping your hand on the rudder to direct your boat there, you could potentially end up anywhere in the ocean. That is why focus and effort are needed to keep you on track. If you give up a few miles into your journey and let go of the rudder you can't expect to arrive where you wanted to go. You must commit to your new destination and keep a hand on the rudder, and eventually you will arrive. 'Begin with the end in mind', as Stephen Covey says in *The 7 Habits of Highly Effective People* (Covey, 2004).

Many people end up not achieving their goals because they lose focus or do not see results quickly enough, then give up. You cannot really expect to change your life without any effort or input. Life is a journey, as they say, and it is not always the destination that is important but sometimes the journey itself. Remember that if you keep doing what you have always done you will keep getting what you have always got. When we think of our life it can feel overwhelming to try and change. That is why we focus on small, manageable steps – one step at a time, which is always in reach.

When things feel too big to handle, just take one step at a time.

THE GROW MODEL (WHITMORE, 2002)

There is a model called the GROW model, attributed to Sir John Whitmore, that has been adapted many times from the original and may help you when setting goals. The letters stand for Goal, Reality, Options and Will, and it is a very simple model to remember.

The GROW model provides a structure to help move a conversation/idea through to a place of motivated action. This is very helpful when, as an individual, you do not always have the answers to your own questions. The process is most helpful when something needs to be achieved or a situation moved forward, and can often prevent a stalemate situation.

Figure 9.1: GROW model

GROW

Goal

The first question you need to ask yourself is, 'What is the outcome I am looking for? What do I want to achieve?' Goals need to be **SMART** (Specific, Measurable, Achievable, Realistic and Timed). Make sure that the goal is realistic and achievable. It could be a short-, medium- or long-term goal. If a goal is too big then it needs to be broken down into logical chunks. If possible, you need to stretch yourself just out of your comfort zone to set a new baseline on which to build. Choose one of your goals from your wheel of life.

Reality

The next step is to encourage yourself to fully explore and describe the situation as it is now. This can take the most amount of time and deserves the biggest part of questioning. Ask yourself questions such as, 'What is my reality like now?' And, 'What's happening now?' Say it aloud or write it down. This is important because when things are just in our head we are not as clear as we need to be. This may need to be discussed before the goal is set, but make sure you go back to establishing a clear goal before moving on.

Options

This is the fun part where you can begin to think up all the ways you could possibly achieve what you would like to do. Try to use some happy, creative thinking as often crazy, funny ideas can free up the creative side of the brain to come up with more rational solutions. Write down all the options as you think of them and try to create at least five. When you have thoroughly explored all the options that would help you to achieve your goal, you can then begin to narrow them down to a few that can realistically take you forward into action. Options can range from small to large things to do – the important thing is that action is taking place. Any action is better than no action.

Will

The final part involves nailing down the detail of which option you are going to make happen. This will need effort and commitment to follow it through. What might you need to make it happen? What resources will help you? Time, materials, friends, help, encouragement? Check again that this is realistic. Ask yourself what could get in the way of it happening and if there is anything that you need to do. Finally, agree with yourself a timeframe in which it will be done so that you can check your progress.

 REFLECTION

When you have this information, you need to ask yourself a couple of serious questions: 'Will going after this goal and achieving it be fair to those that are closest to me? Will it take me towards where I want to be?' This is important as we can often get caught up in things that are nice or attractive but, ultimately, are not helping us get to where we want to go. Are the goals in line with your values?

 LIST YOUR GOALS FOR EACH SEGMENT OF YOUR LIFE

List your goals for each segment of your life, then use the GROW model for each step to turn it into a SMART goal with a clear timeframe. You should have around eight clear goals to work on and each one should end up with a clear action. Small and doable is better than big and overwhelming. Be patient and kind to yourself.

In addition, you can use a goal-setting timeline to create the overview of your new future. You could use a stepping-stone timeline like the template given in Figure 9.2. The idea is that you describe your overall goal at the end and put a realistic date that you want to achieve it by. Then you can plot the mini goals, the small steps along the timeline, that you will need to do to take you there. Alongside you can write down any resources that you will need and who could help you. It is good to print this out and stick it up on your fridge or beside your bed so that every morning and evening you can review it to remain focused. This helps embed the pathway in your brain to help you achieve it. Your brain can then alert

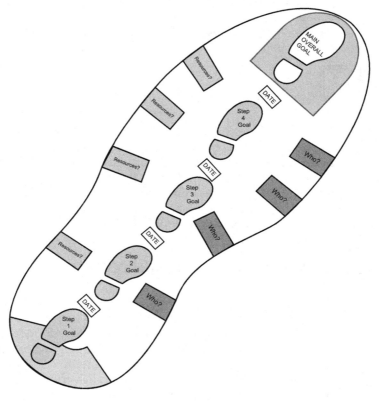

Figure 9.2: Goal stepping stones

you to opportunities that may help you to achieve your goal that you may never have noticed before.

There is so much information that is streaming into our brains, it often has to filter out a great deal of irrelevant information while noticing what will be helpful to us. If our brains did not do this, we could become seriously overloaded in our thinking. However, once you have set a pathway for your brain it can then allow information through to your conscious that could be helpful. An example could be that a friend buys a certain make and model of car that you have never really noticed before. Your brain has filtered it out as being irrelevant. Now that your brain knows about it, it starts to look out for this type of car and alert you when it sees one rather than filtering it out as just another car.

Start small and be clear about your short-, medium- and long-term goals.

Motivation and contingency planning

INTRODUCTION

This Step explores how motivation is created in people. It focuses on helping you identify your own ways of being motivated, along with what may be outside of your control and the importance of having a contingency plan.

Congratulations on getting to Step 10. While the goal setting is important, so is understanding the motivation to get you there. Rewards along the way can be crucial, so if you are someone that is more motivated by reward, then factor this in when you are planning. Some people are either motivated by the carrot or the stick. Neither is right or wrong, but it is helpful to know which you are motivated by.

MOTIVATED BY THE STICK

Think of a long railway line with the 'pain station' at one end and the 'pleasure station' at the other end. You could be a train parked at the pain station, and when things become too painful for you to bear, you will pull out of the station and start to chug along the track away from pain. You want things to change as they have become too much to cope with. However, as you go along the track and move further away from the place of pain, you realise that things are less painful and you start to slow down. Your motivation begins to wane. The effort you put in is less, so the train starts to slide back down the track towards the pain station again. This is ok for a while until very soon the train slides right back to the pain station. After a short time, the pain gets too much to bear

DOI: 10.4324/9781003172734-10

again so, once more, you pull out of the station and start to chug along the line. If this sounds like you then you will need to remind yourself how painful it will be if you do not keep going. What will be the down sides of not achieving your goal? What will the negative impact be on you and your life if you do not act?

MOTIVATED BY THE CARROT

If you are someone that is motivated by positive things and rewards you may find it easier to keep focused on the result. It is also great to reward yourself along the way and congratulate yourself on how far you have come. Your train will be going along the track towards the pleasure station. It will be the thought of the reward at the end or along the way that keeps you going. The train will be constantly pulling you towards the wonderful 'prize' at the end. If this sounds like you then you need to make sure that you have enough rewards dotted along the way to keep you motivated to keep going. You can write up all the reasons you want to have this new way of life. What are the benefits? What will it do for you? What will you get as a result? Keep them posted up so that you can keep focused on the reasons why this is pleasurable and important.

 REFLECTION

Think about what has motivated you to get this far through this workbook. Begin to recognise how you are motivated and remain aware of how you might trip yourself up. Put in place ways of keeping your motivation going – perhaps by rewards at each successful step or by notes posted up of how painful it would be to not do anything.

CONTINGENCY

It is helpful to recognise that you do not have control over every aspect of your life. Sometimes things do go wrong and that is just the way life is. Many things that happen are just out of our control. The important bit is how you deal with it by not being too hard on yourself so that you remain resilient. It is worth thinking through what you could do as a contingency plan if the first step of your goal does not work out. Earlier in my life I seemed to be set back by challenge after challenge. I could have adopted the victim mindset and felt that the whole world was against me. Instead, I decided to frame each experience as if the higher powers were testing me out for resilience and tenacity. I was determined not to be put off and if one door metaphorically did not open then I would try other ways of achieving the same thing. Listen to your heart and try to stay in touch with what is right for you, and don't give up if you believe it to be the right thing.

A NEW RELATIONSHIP

'What me – you must be joking!!', some of you may be thinking. 'After all I have been through, I would rather stick pins in my eyes or walk through a bed of nettles naked!' I have a great theory that we meet the people who will teach us most about ourselves. What this means is that in every relationship we have, when our 'buttons' are pressed it is actually highlighting an opportunity for us to learn something about ourselves. I appreciate this may be difficult to swallow at this early stage, but we can always learn from our experiences. In every interaction or communication that elicits a strong feeling or response within us, it highlights there may be an opportunity for learning something about ourselves. I have noticed most reactions that are negative are driven out of fear. If we can pinpoint what we think we are afraid of, we can then begin to recognise whether our reaction or behaviour is appropriate for the situation. You may have had reactions that are triggered by fear or insecurity at some level. It is important to try and understand for yourself where these reactions are coming from and ask yourself if they are appropriate. If you feel you are still struggling with this, I recommend seeking out some sessions with a psychotherapist. The important thing is to be open to learning about yourself so you can grow and develop from situations and see your own value. My learning has helped me in a new relationship to see that it is possible to be loved and respected, but I had to start to love and respect myself again first. Do not forget your list of values, which you can compare with those of a potential new partner!

Your value isn't determined by how others behave towards you.

Self-care

This chapter offers an overview of self-care and why it is so important. While a whole book could be written about this topic, and many have, I have tried to outline the principles that will be most useful to you. Please do use this as a springboard to explore further and maybe start by changing one small habit in your life that will make the biggest difference to your wellbeing.

WHAT IS SELF-CARE?

In a nutshell, my definition of self-care is the awareness and ability to know what our mind and bodies need to regenerate and keep us functioning as healthy human beings. The four areas of self-care to focus on are our mental, physical, emotional and spiritual wellbeing.

WHY IS SELF-CARE IMPORTANT?

Now more than ever the emphasis is on the need for self-care. The recent pandemic has focused everyone's minds on how important it is to not only maintain our physical health but also our mental health. Often when people are in a relationship, they are very good at being and doing things in support of other people. However, it is easy to lose touch with valuing ourselves enough to take the appropriate level of physical and mental care that we need to stay well. We normally learn how to look after ourselves from our parents and those that care for us, but if for any reason this has been lacking, we may not know how best to look after ourselves.

DOI: 10.4324/9781003172734-11

The daily pressures of life in a modern society can also have a detrimental effect on our wellbeing – partly as 'we' have created a world where we are accessible 24/7 via social media, technology and even our watches, and also because of the multitude of everyday tasks that we are asked to juggle. We are now living in a world that enables interaction and judgement between us every day and night on a global scale. However, the natural rhythms that our bodies and minds need to function as a human being have not evolved in line with the scale of communication that is now available to us.

This can become a problem when the balance between output and input begins to tip and we no longer take the time and care we need to keep ourselves healthy. Think of the analogy that if you are in an aeroplane and a situation arises that causes the oxygen masks to drop from the ceiling, you have to put your own oxygen mask on first. When we think of this analogy in daily life, it makes complete sense: without looking after ourselves first it becomes impossible to help anyone else. Spending some time looking after yourself is no more selfish then eating or drinking.

Without being glib, I have met and coached many people that somehow assume their head is not attached to their body. That for some reason their thinking, motivation and drive is all that they listen to, expecting their body to keep up without any thought of maintenance. Ignoring the needs of your body can create a risk of 'burnout' and often manifests in people getting ill just when they stop work and are ready to go on holiday. While this may sound obvious and a bit silly, it is important to remember that your head and your body work as a whole system in collaboration with each other. Like a car, you can only expect it to keep running for the life-time expectancy by servicing it regularly and renewing its consumables. It is no good to just keep programming your sat nav if you do not check that you have enough fuel in your tank or oil in your engine to continually make journeys.

Naturally and historically our bodies would have periods of rest and activity. Being mindful of how our bodies would naturally want to act can help us keep in touch with what may be best for us. Most mammals will rest after eating a meal, allowing their bodies time to physically digest the food, repair and re-energise before getting back to a period of activity. Our natural rhythm involves periods of expending energy balanced with periods of rest.

If we ignore the body's natural desire for the right amount of sleep, the most nutritious food, hydration, the rest and relaxation that our brains and bodies need, we start to deplete the body of its ability to regenerate and maintain stability in its own system. This can then lead to a poor physical state, low mood, a lack of positive energy and poor decision making – all contributing to a sense of a mental and physical downward spiral and potential illness.

To that end, it is helpful to bring this area back into perspective for ourselves as part of this journey. To remain healthy and to continue to make the best decisions for ourselves, we need to factor in focusing on self-care as a matter of routine.

Loehr and Schwartz (2003) did an enormous amount of work researching how athletes could perform at their best. They then transferred this learning into the workplace for those in professional positions, supporting them to perform effectively and efficiently over long periods of time, even their whole career. The term they used is 'corporate athletes'. While many of us do not need to be corporate athletes, the principles of their research are useful in helping us understand what we can focus on to keep us as healthy as possible.

THE FOUR DIMENSIONS OF SELF-CARE

The four dimensions of self-care are all interlinked to create our overall wellbeing. They all need to be connected and interact with each other for us to be as healthy and effective as we can.

If we are not physically well our emotional and mental wellbeing will suffer. Equally, if we are not at our best emotionally and mentally our physical wellbeing is likely to suffer.

If we are not happy or 'at ease' in our minds, it can create 'dis-ease' in our bodies. The aim is to keep a realistic balance between all four dimensions to the best of our ability within the circumstances we have. We are not aiming for perfection but rather to make small changes that we can consistently maintain and build on to keep ourselves healthy, functioning and at ease.

Mental

Looking after ourselves mentally takes mental energy. This area is about our ability to hold our thoughts and concentration on the tasks we are doing and, in addition, to train our brain to help us rather than hinder us. In modern society we are very used to instantaneous reward and reaction, and therefore holding concentration and working towards a positive outcome or solution can be much harder to do. We can give up easily or feel we do not have the energy to stay focused. Here are some thoughts on how you can improve your focus and thinking to support you more fully.

Have personal boundaries

Much of our mental energy can be drained by negativity. Decide what your personal boundaries need to be. An example may be deciding you will no longer tolerate being spoken to in a way that is not kind or supportive (including how you speak to yourself). Once you have identified that your boundary is being crossed, you have choices. You could decide to shut the conversation down and walk away. This could be an opportunity to practise your assertiveness skills by calmly stating that the way you are being spoken to is making you feel uncomfortable and that maybe it is best to take a break and talk about it later. Maintain mental energy by choosing not to be involved in running other people down or criticising others. Choose to hold someone's confidence and tell no one else if they trust in you. These are your own personal boundaries that you can hold and live up to. Have a contract with yourself at some level regarding how you are going to look after your boundaries and what you expect of yourself. You may not always be able to hold them, but it is work in progress. The key is to be forgiving of your-self if negative patterns still happen. Be generous to yourself that you have noticed and are working on them.

Solution thinking

Solution thinking is just that. Creating a mindset in which when you are experiencing a problem you start to think about how many solutions there may be and what you could do to resolve it. Focusing on a problem has been found to create a threat response internally, which limits our creativity. Seeing problems as interesting challenges to overcome rather than barriers or walls that are insurmountable can help create a feeling of empowerment rather than one of being a victim. You will be surprised how many solutions you can come up with. It can even become fun. It doesn't mean you have to do them or even that you like them, but simply that you recog-nise that choices are there.

Brain training

There are some great apps for smartphones and on the internet for brain training. Fun games and puzzles that will help you to keep your mind active, engaged and learning. Learning new skills has been proven to use parts of our brain that have been previously dormant. This is healthy for the brain as it creates new neural pathways that previously didn't exist. Recent findings dictate that for the brain, 90 minutes of focused work is the optimum amount of time before needing to take a minimum of a 15-minute break. After this period, it has been found that you retain very little of the information you are trying to remember.

Optimism

Realistic optimism is helpful to maintain a sense of hope about any situation. This isn't suggesting that you reject your/the current reality but that you accept how it is now while maintaining hope by working towards a preferred future or outcome that you can influence.

Quiet time

When I talk about quiet time, I mean time that allows your thinking brain to switch off and have a rest. Often our best ideas come when we have given our brain some quiet time to allow whatever bright ideas it has to filter up from our subconscious. When we are busy thinking in our conscious mind, we are not allowing space for our brain to solve our problems. As an example, I often start to calm down when I have just got into bed and then my brain suddenly flags up to me that I should have phoned someone, or I remember something important. This is frustrating as the timing may not be good. I am learning that allowing some quiet time in the day provides space for my brain to offer things that may be of help to me. We often rate and value 'doing' something more highly than just 'being', but from my experience we can be the most effective when these two areas are balanced. It may be worth checking out your beliefs around doing nothing, as if you believe that sitting quietly is being lazy, this may inhibit your ability to allow for quiet time.

Emotional

The difference between emotions and feelings can be complex. That said, emotion is the body creating a reaction to a situation and telling the brain, which then creates a response as a feeling. Two people can have the same emotion but attach a different feeling to it. For example, the emotion could be fear, but the feeling could be excited or scared. The seven basic emotions that we all feel are anger, fear, disgust, happiness, sadness, surprise and contempt.

We all have emotions, and they are all there for a reason. It is helpful to know which emotions are creating the feelings we have, rather than just acting out our feelings through behaviour. To be emotionally well-balanced it is helpful to recognise and process the emotions that we are feeling or holding on to. Some believe that our bodies store negative emotions, and if that is so then one way of looking at this is that the emotion will be maintained inside us until it can find a way of expressing itself. If we are not acknowledging how we are feeling, the emotion can come out at an inappropriate moment. For example, if you were feeling sad that your dog had died but had not allowed yourself to cry or grieve, you could then be sat around a table having a meal with friends where someone else was feeling sad and said something sad, which may then trigger you into tears without others knowing why. On the flipside, some people become emotionally detached from their feelings to protect themselves from the pain. Different people process emotions differently and there is no right or wrong way. You may hear someone say, 'I think', rather than, 'I feel'. They are both important to us and everyone will have a mix of both. It is helpful to try to use your rational mind to think things through while also not losing touch with your emotional side. Other people, however, may process their experience much more through emotions and feelings. If not balanced with a rational side, the negative effects of being very emotional about everything can become very draining.

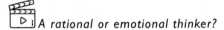 *A rational or emotional thinker?*

Think about whether you lean more towards rational thinking or emotional thinking and then try to devise a strategy to help your own awareness.

Self-awareness

For us to make personal changes we need to first develop our ability to notice our own reactions, thoughts and feelings. Until you stand back and observe yourself objectively, it can be very hard to change your thinking and behaviour. Start to notice your emotions/feelings and identify them. Are you happy, sad, angry, etc.? If you recognise you are feeling sad or lonely or angry, just step back and try to understand why this feeling is occurring. It may be obvious, but sometimes we have what are called primary and secondary emotions. For example, I may be feeling and presenting as angry (as a secondary emotion), but actually underneath I am feeling very fearful (a primary emotion). How is the feeling trying to help you? What can you do or say from the adult part of you that will give you a better result? It is very difficult when we are in an emotion or feeling to step outside of ourselves and notice that we are in a behaviour. However, if you can start to notice, you may be able to change your normal response or just pause things to give yourself time to think about what a better approach may be. Being hungry is a great example. I notice that when I am hungry I am often more short-tempered and grumpier – I think the current expression is hangry! A cross between hungry and angry. When I can notice this about myself, I can then do something about it by finding some food. If I have noticed in time, I may not need to apologise to those around me! Go back to Step 2 to see the model.

 Body scan

Sit quietly and scan your body for any feelings you may be holding on to. Is there tightness in your shoulders or tension in your thighs or back? Where in your body are you holding on to something? What might this feeling be trying to tell you? Listening to our bodies is a useful tool to align our health and wellbeing.

 Rewind

Think about a situation that you felt you could have handled better. What would you want to do differently next time? How will you notice so that you can do it differently? What sense in your body will you feel first that will tell you something is not right for you?

Physical

Diet

A balanced diet is well known for positive health benefits. This includes the right amount of fruit, vegetables, carbohydrates, proteins, fats, vitamins and minerals to keep all our working organs, tissue, bones, brain, skin, and so on, working as effectively as possible. Even minute deficits of essential minerals and vitamins can negatively impact our thinking and the body's ability to repair its cells and tissues.

Incorporating fresh fruit and vegetables into your diet daily is not only a great way of getting fibre to support your digestive system but also provides precious antioxidants, which help in the prevention of cancer and other diseases. Another key to good health is remaining hydrated. Our bodies need a good supply of clean fresh water every day to keep our systems working effectively. Make sure you are hydrated by drinking enough water throughout the day.

Some points to think about include:

- Eat at regular mealtimes to help maintain and stabilise blood sugar levels, which can affect your mood and outlook on life.
- Rest after a meal to allow your body and mind some downtime to successfully digest the food you have eaten, and for your mind to digest and process the events up to that point in the day.
- Keep hydrated throughout the day by drinking the recommended amount of water.
- Maintain or aim for the right weight for your height and build, as this can reduce your risk of heart disease and diabetes, put less strain on your joints and, more recently, has been shown to reduce the risk of complications from Covid-19. Being overweight has been shown to increase wear and tear on your joints, such as knees and hips, and increase the likelihood of needing knee or hip replacements.
- Use as many natural products as possible. This reduces the risk of absorbing chemicals from topical products, such as moisturisers, body lotions and anti-perspirants, into your system.
- Avoid alcohol. While many of us can appreciate the temporary feeling of relaxation that alcohol brings, it is also a known depressant. Drinking alcohol regularly, even in moderate amounts, can create a feeling of low mood and despondency as well as affect sleep patterns.

Exercise

There is no shortage of information supporting the benefits of exercise for our mind and body, but a few general points may help. Our heart is a muscle and, like all muscles, only remains strong if it is exercised regularly. Raising our heart rate makes our heart pump more strongly, taking blood and oxygen around our bodies to replenish our organs, muscles, lungs and brain. Exercise keeps our muscles, ligaments and tendons strong and more toned, which in turn reduces our risk of injury from normal everyday activity, all while releasing 'feel good' endorphins into our blood stream. These 'feel good hormones' are responsible for that post-workout mental high.

 **Move more**

Whether it's starting with just a fast walk a day and building on this to a regular routine, try and build up to and incorporate at least 20 minutes of heartbeat-raising exercise three times a week, as a minimum, to support your physical and mental health. This could be a fast walk from the car to your place of work, taking the stairs instead of the lift or even exercising in your own living room.

Breathing

Breathing is good! Without it you would not make it to the bottom of the page. But how we breathe can also make an enormous difference to our thinking, our wellbeing and our physical state. Our breathing is a direct link between our body and brain. If we are afraid, sense danger or are becoming stressed, our breathing will become shallow. We can tell this as it will only be the top part of our chest that is moving. The oxygen will travel to maintain our main organs ready for a fight, flight or freeze response, and we may feel faint or lightheaded. If our bodies and minds are in a state of defensiveness, even when there is not any logical threat, we are likely to create an inner state of 'dis-ease'. Therefore, one of the most effective and easiest actions to calm our body and brains down is to take time to concentrate on our breathing daily. Breathing deeply for a few minutes at a time can reduce your anxiety and threat response. You can also do this if you are feeling anxious at any time without knowing the reason. Slowing your breathing down signals to the body that there is no threat present and therefore it does not need to prepare for a fight, flight or freeze response, and can instead relax. Take time to notice your breathing throughout the day. The more under pressure you feel the more likely you are to start to breathe in a shallow way.

 Breathe!

Every few hours focus on your breathing and if you feel you are stressed or breathing faster than normal then take a moment to try this exercise. Breathe in to the count of five, through your nose and deep down into your diaphragm. Hold for the count of five and then breathe out through your mouth to the count of five. Repeat this for a few minutes.

Sleep patterns

Many people are affected by either a lack of sleep or sleep patterns that they feel are not helpful to them. The recommended amount of sleep is an average of 7 hours per night, but this does vary slightly in either direction depending on who you are, your age and what your lifestyle dictates. When thinking about what is best for you it can help to think about what your body would do naturally. Some basic thoughts to aid good sleep are:

- Remain in tune with the natural world in terms of making it as dark as possible when going to bed and getting up in the day light when possible.
- Avoid alcohol because, while this often induces a heavy sleep initially, it can then interrupt and create light sleeping patterns intermittently for the rest of the night.
- Relax with a warm bath or shower and calm environment at least an hour before going to bed.
- Leave all phones and social media, and any electronic interruptions, outside of the bedroom and give yourself at least half an hour off them before sleeping. If you do use

your phone as an alarm, some phones can still be turned onto mute without affecting this. You could turn it upside down and leave it on a surface that won't vibrate, such as a carpet.

- Keep your room as dark and quiet as possible.
- Take as much exercise as you can in the day. It isn't rocket science to realise if you do enough exercise to get physically tired you are likely to have a better quality of sleep.
- Reduce any anxieties or issues that are playing on your mind by writing them down in a journal before going to bed. If possible, think up one action that would help resolve the issue and write this down. Then forget about it for that night.
- Using one drop of lavender oil in a purpose-built lamp or oil burner can help some people sleep more soundly. (Be very careful to read all instructions and directions as too much oil can have a profoundly opposite effect).
- Reading a nice book while in bed can often help you relax from the day and help you to feel sleepy.
- Being mindful of what you are watching or listening to before bedtime can also have a positive or negative effect. Try not to watch or listen to the news or anything negative or distressing before going to sleep.
- Stick to a routine of going to bed at the same time every night and getting up at the same time every morning.

Spiritual/purpose

The word 'spiritual' will have different meanings for different individuals. What I mean by this is connection and purpose. For some people this is a religion that they have chosen to believe in. For others it is about being connected to something bigger than themselves and having a purpose outside of their own needs. This could be believing that you are on the planet for a reason or just being connected to like-minded people and helping others.

 Helping others

What skills and qualities do you have that can help others? For example, are you a good listener? Do you like doing odd jobs or gardening? Some people love cleaning. It may be that you can find opportunities to help others locally and increase your own sense of purpose and value.

Volunteering in some form for your community to help others can give you a real sense of value and purpose. Often when we give things without any expectation of gaining something in return it can make us feel good about ourselves and life. Thinking about others in the community and how we can help support them can equally give ourselves a sense of wellbeing. It is a win–win.

 *Sense of purpose*

Write down the things you could do that would help others, and in turn support your sense of purpose.

Social interaction

Keeping in touch with friends and social groups is important. By this I do not necessarily mean through social media but physical groups that you can be in touch with that are like-minded and where you feel understood and accepted for who you are. Social interaction is proving to be more difficult with the Covid-19 pandemic, but if you can find someone and be in a support bubble with each other it can support your mental health.

SUMMARY

I have learned many hard lessons in life, mostly by being exposed to challenging situations. In any given situation we can make choices about how we want to react to it, view it, perceive it, sometimes even experience it. I have always tried to take some learning from whatever has happened to me and use it as a positive influence in my life. This has helped me in that I have rarely considered myself a victim. Rather than feeling that way, I have come to embrace situations that can teach me something about myself. When I was young (even though it may have been a survival strategy), I framed experiences as challenges that were being sent to me to make me stronger, as if they were a test to see if I could overcome them. I fantasised that it was some kind of 'higher order' gauging if I had the courage and morals to do the right thing and show what I was made of. But I never quite knew what I was being primed for! At some point I learned that stress is healthy, and it is only by being in a state of stress that we can expand our capacity to manage stressful situations. The important bit is that the stress is not prolonged, therefore giving ourselves time for rest and recovery after the stressful event. We will then have expanded our own capacity to manage stressful situations as a part of life. As a society I am concerned that we are led to believe we should never have to suffer any pain. In my view, it is unrealistic to expect to get through life without any physical or emotional pain. These very experiences are what shape our lives and personalities. They make us resilient and wise.

One of the greatest life-changing techniques I have learned is to train my brain to focus on what I DO want. Even when I am in situations that are no longer healthy for me, I try to keep visualising and focusing on the metaphorical horizon of where I want to get to. This technique has turned my life around 180 degrees – from one of a difficult relationship, not living in a good environment or in a property I wanted to be in, with finances that were a struggle, in a job I didn't like, to a life with a loving relationship, in a place I love, doing something that is important, to not only myself but in support of others, and financially ok. I am not sharing this to 'look good' but, on the contrary, to offer hope, in that if I can turn my life around from one of despair and desperation, then you can to. Yes, it does take patience and time. There is no obvious end to the journey, and it is part of your life's work. But it does happen: slowly, methodically and built on a firm and strong foundation, creating a new, authentic future in line with who you are.

Life is a journey and being open to our own growth and development as a human being is a unique opportunity, one I feel is crucial to our time here. With this workbook I wanted to share some of the learning and development I have found to be so helpful in getting my own life on track. Take one step at a time and acknowledge that you may have setbacks, and that is ok. You can go back to any part of this workbook and review it when you need to. One of the biggest support groups anyone can have on their personal journey is their close friends. If you have someone you can rely on, then share your journey with them. If you don't, then maybe set a goal of friendship with someone who has the same values as you. If you feel inclined, then explore the possibility of finding yourself a personal coach that can be with you every step of the way and support you when you need it most. A good coach will remain non-judgemental and have your best interests at heart, as well as being able to keep your plans realistic and achievable. Make sure they are accredited, insured and have regular supervision. Seek the help you need. You are a wonderful human being. You deserve love, kindness, happiness. I truly wish you all the best for your journey and your new life. If you get stuck, ask yourself the question, 'What would I advise someone else to do?'

Well done for exploring this workbook and opening your mind to possibility. All change takes courage and I believe in you! Congratulations on taking your first 10 steps towards designing your new future.

With love, Dee
Dartmoor 2021

References

Cambridge Online Dictionary. (n.d.). Retrieved from https://dictionary.cambridge.org/dictionary/english/belief?q=beliefs. Accessed October 2020.

Church, D. (2018). *Mind to Matter*. London: Hay House UK.

Covey, S. (2004). *The 7 Habits of Highly Effective People*. London: Simon & Schuster.

Curran, A. (2008). *The Little Book of Big Stuff About the Brain*. Wales: Crown House Publishing.

Henwood, S. (2014). *Practical Leadership in Nursing and Health Care*. Oxon: Taylor & Francis.

Mascaro, J. (1973). *The Dhammapada*. London: Penguin Books.

Meyer, P. J. (1960). *Success Motivation Institute*. https://www.successmotivation.co.nz/paul-j-meyer/

Livehappy.com. (2020). Retrieved from livehappy.com. Accessed January 2021.

Loehr, J. and Schwartz, T. (2003). *On Form*. London: Nicholas Brealey Publishing.

Perry, M. (2004). *Confidence Booster Workout*. San Diego, CA: Octopus Publishing Group.

Rock, D. (2009). *Your Brain At Work*. New York: Harper Collins.

Whitmore, J. (2002). *Coaching for Performance* (3rd ed.). London: Nicholas Brealey Publishing.

Wilkinson, D. (2012). *Goal Setting Made Easy*. Amazon (self-published). Retrieved from https://www.amazon.co.uk/Goal-Setting-Made-Easy-Wilkinson-ebook/dp/B008B8682M/ref=sr_1_3?dchild=1&keywords=goal+setting+made+easy&qid=1624269467&sr=8-3.

Recommendations

Domestic abuse help information

British Psychological Society	www.bps.org.uk
National Domestic Abuse Helpline	www.nationaldahelpline.org.uk
Refuge	www.refuge.org.uk

United Kingdom Government	https://www.gov.uk/guidance/domestic-abuse-how-to-get-help
Women's Aid Federation of England	www.womensaid.org.uk

Coaching support and finding a coach

European Mentoring and Coaching Council	www.emccglobal.org
International Coaching Federation	www.coachfederation.org
South West Coaching	www.southwestcoaching.co.uk

Printed in the United States
by Baker & Taylor Publisher Services